THE VERANDAH POEMS

THE
VERANDAH
POEMS

JEAN 'BINTA' BREEZE

WITH PHOTOGRAPHS BY
TEHRON ROYES

BLOODAXE BOOKS

Poems copyright © Jean 'Binta' Breeze 2016
Photographs © Tehron Royes 2015, 2016
Foreword © Kei Miller 2016

ISBN: 978 1 78037 285 3

First published 2016 by
Bloodaxe Books Ltd,
Eastburn,
South Park,
Hexham,
Northumberland NE46 1BS.

www.bloodaxebooks.com
For further information about Bloodaxe titles
please visit our website or write to
the above address for a catalogue.

Supported using public funding by
ARTS COUNCIL
ENGLAND

Cover design: Neil Astley & Pamela Robertson-Pearce.

Printed in Great Britain by Bell & Bain Limited, Glasgow, Scotland, on
acid-free paper sourced from mills with FSC chain of custody certification.

CONTENTS

THE VERANDAH MATTERS

They jut out like tongues from the mouths of houses – verandahs, I mean. And I sometimes wonder if the original designers had this in mind – the image of the mouth, the simple act of talk, the complex bonding of people and communities – when they drew them.

Verandah. Or Veranda – without an 'h' – though never in Jamaica. In Jamaica we almost always spell it with an 'h'. The origin however is a Hindi word, *varanda*. It seems then that this roofed porch, this open gallery that extends from the house like a tongue, originates in the Indian subcontinent. The colonial project displaces not only people, but trees, and animals, and architectural features. The verandah has travelled to other hot climates – to Australia, to the Southern United States, all across the Caribbean – an important feature before the invention of Air Conditioning.

In all these regions, Australia, the American South, the Caribbean, the verandah goes native – becomes part of what designers would call 'vernacular architecture', traditional, local. But what a helpful double meaning that is – vernacular architecture – for once again we think of language, the image of the mouth, the simple act of talk and the complex bonding of people and communities.

Verandahs matter. They matter deeply. And yes, I do mean to invoke that other phrase. For in these tumultuous times when events across the world have reminded us that 'Black Lives Matter', we might pause to think about those places where such lives are often narrated – are narrated with such care, with such empathy, and with such insight, that it might seem that these are the places where Black Lives happen.

The verandah matters in life and in literature. We know this from as far back as Zora Neale Hurston's brilliant novel *Their Eyes Were Watching God*. When Janie returns, she finds the community outside, sitting empowered on their porches.

> It was the time for sitting on porches beside the road. It was the time to hear things and talk. These sitters had been tongueless, earless, eyeless conveniences all day long. Mules and other brutes had occupied their skins. But now,

the sun and the bossman were gone, so the skins felt power-
ful and human. They became lords of sounds and lesser
things. They passed nations through their mouths. [pp.1-2]

In Hurston's novel, Janie tells her own story to Phoebe on her
back porch, but we also travel to the front porch of the store and
hear the community telling several other stories.

In the wonderful poems that make up this collection, the Jam-
aican poet, Jean 'Binta' Breeze, has created yet another verandah.
From it we can see the Caribbean Sea; we can see the bar across
the road, its large screen TV showing football matches; we can see
a whole Jamaican community – the people who walk by, who
occasionally stop to come and sit down with the poet, in their
own ways becoming lords of sounds and lesser things.

The poet invites us over to her verandah as well. Here we can
relax. Here we can listen to stories that matter. Here we can take
a small respite from the heat of our day to lives. Here, on this
verandah, (and this is exactly how we would say it in Jamaica) we
can sit back and catch a little Breeze.

KEI MILLER

THE VERANDAH POEMS

PRIMING

Next week is New Year's Eve
one whole year pass
since I been priming you

Not a day gone by
and I don't think of what to bring you
no night pass
and I don't dream
of how I want to touch you

First thing in the morning
I pick you up
8 o'clock on the dot
and I take you to the beach
for your morning swim
I don't sit in the car
and read newspaper
no
I swim with you
200 butterfly
200 crawl
and any number of breast stroke
till we get tired

I talk to you
till you get your breath
then sit with you in the sun
watch you go golden brown
and then I drive you home
to have your shower

That's not priming?
if it was my car
I would change every spark plug

fill the radiator with water
and change the oil
and then I would get in it
and drive

but you
after all the priming
one year of mornings on the beach
and not even a kiss
have to beg for a hug
you is the hardest woman I ever prime

and then lunchtime
I bring your vegetable soup
from the rastaman up at Great River
make your inside as clean as your sunshine skin

and still not allowed to touch
this priming not working
is the longest I ever prime a woman
and get nothing out of it

I am back again in the evening
take you to drink a cold beer
to eat fish and bammy by the sea
hoping to melt you down
hoping to tune your engine
to the right pitch
so I could drive you home

but you jump out the car
quick quick
as we reach your gate
quick kiss (no tongue you say)
quick hug
and through your door

Goodnight Philip you say

A year of priming
no results
all that hard work
for nothing

A woman never make me work so long
think I have to find another one
that's easier to prime
but when I tell you that
you say
Philip
you find me on my verandah
breathing in the sea
comfortably
and you can leave me
on my verandah
drinking in the sea
comfortably
but sex is not for me
and no amount of priming
will let you enter me

STRANGER

A stranger walked in off the road today
that can't be helped
with the gate wide open
and the short railings
no grills, no locks

this is not Kingston
this is countryside, Jamaica

he is polite
this stranger
any dawg, mam?
no dawg, sir

I could clean your car, mam
no car sir
I could scour your awnings
we do that ourselves

Don't think I'm always like this, mam
I need bus fare to reach home
Grange Hill is two bus ride away

I am trying to find my baby mother
I took that woman in
with three children
from three different men
I feed and school them
and then she had two more for me

and five years later
one of the baby father
came home from 'merica
every morning quarrel

and every night fight
till she stabbed me in the eye

I walked the street crying
been walking three years
working where I could
but now I need bus fare
for the children called yesterday
say she need some help
and for them
I'll try again

so just a bus fare
for not every man is a dawg
no mam
not every man is a dawg
if you have children
you know what I mean
not every man is a dawg

He leaves me on the verandah
leaves with my last fifty dollars
leaves me
with the two sides of the story

HOME WORK

Aneisha comes on Thursdays
to do the ironing
when it gets too hot in the laundry room
she sits on my verandah

Today I am complaining
about how much it costs
to keep my daughter in university
she says
but ma'am
it's de maddas dat I hear complaining
I never hear de man dem talk
bout how much for school fees
years after we done breastfeeding
it's like it never stops
it's like it never stops

A slight breeze touches us from off the sea
the leaves on the mango tree stir
I say
it is not their fault
we open our legs willingly
and the children come easily
and the fathers left as quickly
as they came
she says

all we can do is take a little breeze
in the midday sun
and never forget
there's more work to be done

She rises to her feet
well, the clothes won't iron themselves
poems won't write themselves either
I return

EVENING

Evening brings its conversations
it's just becoming dark
and as usual
the red jeep turns into the driveway
blocking the last vision of the sea
Philip brings the first fruits of the season
naseberries, mangoes, custard apples

If there is nothing on the road today
he suggests an ice cold beer
which he pops across the road for
he does not come to the verandah
without bearing gifts
and these gifts start the conversation

Today he brings my beer cold
his is hot
the bartender told him
his headache is a sign of low blood pressure
and a hot beer will put paid to that

I say, why don't you see the doctor
before it is too late
he says he'll go tomorrow
I know he won't
it will take several reminders

Philip is into bush
for his nerves
it's sour sop leaf tea
neem is the cure for diabetes
and the present miracle bush is called
merengeh

He chews the seed
and drinks the leaves in hot tea
every morning

My mother passes by that bit of talk
on her way to water flowers in the front garden
'i will die of something I'm sure
but I won't die of bush,' she says
'you never know how much to take
at least the doctor tells you
one pill a day'
Philip quotes from the Bible
there are herbs he says for all our illnesses
growing right where we are born

My mother seems to have brought the rain
with her watering
there is a thin drizzle in the air
and now the last bit of sunlight has disappeared

Philip says the bartender knows more
than any doctor
his grandmother taught him about herbs
it goes back a long way

Let's take a walk across the road
the rain is not enough to get us wet
the bartender will educate you
and another beer won't hurt

My mother on her way back in hears that too
drinking too much, she says
thought the doctor warned you
ginger beer I say
and signal Philip to shut up

On the edge of the sea
at the bamboo bar
the bartender has the cures
for those who come home
ill from overseas
behind me
the verandah sits empty

FOOTBALL ON THE VERANDAH

It's World Cup 2014
Brazilian fever
rises to a pitch
I must make the choice
between the verandah
with its cool sea breeze
or the TV room
for a closer view of strikers

In England
this would not be a problem
I'd have to be indoors anyway
so football is a welcome treat on TV

but here
to sit inside
at 96 degrees
to look at one small box
in a corner of the room
or to sit on the verandah
with garden, sky and sea

But hold on
blessed are the peacemakers

the bar across the road
has a verandah
looking back at me
and an open window
to their TV

the verandah is full of young fishermen
gathered for the first game
Brazil vs Croatia

I cannot see the screen
it is too small
but the dancing bodies
the groans and screams
tell me all I need to know

I can't see the tears
but I can hear them
an own goal
and Brazil is in despair
so are the young fishermen
who don't believe in underdogs
they want their footballers to be gods

One voice rises above the group
and Jamaican bad words reign
until joy and flying locks
bodies leap from the verandah
on to the edge of the road
stopping traffic for a moment
and Brazil has scored

One all
and all is silent
it seems desperate at times
hands held half way up the head
then let down jerkily
as Croatia tries again and again to score
and then
madness
bedlam
penalty for Brazil
I run inside to watch it
yes – two one – thank God

back on my verandah
after a toilet break

I see one tall young fisherman
dribbling a non-existent ball
down unto the beach
and back
then shoots
the screams are fervent
Brazil has scored again
three-one

I don't believe – not now
no not now
the beer truck has come
to deliver its weekly ration
and parks on the side of the road
between our two verandahs
it leaves its engine running
so not just sight
but sound has gone

I leave my verandah sitting empty
for the heat of the TV room
but even a clear view of the game
cannot bring back the fever of the match

and so it ends
three-one
and Jamaica is hushed on the first day
the love of the ball
the love of Brazil
and an argument all night
as to whether the penalty was fair

A month of this will kill me

THE CASTING OF THE ROOF

My sister is building a house
on one side of the front garden
gone are the hibiscus
the exuria bush that use to feed the hummingbirds
gone are the miniature june plum trees
from which my mother made the juice each week

For the last three weeks
I have watched them
replaced by building blocks and concrete
I have had to reposition my chair
so I do not look directly at the building site
but towards the left side of the garden
which is still blessed
by the julie mango tree
the other small exuria bush
and the oleander

The foreman said last week
they would be casting the roof on Tuesday
I slept an hour late that morning
and came out to the verandah
to find a cement mixer in full swing

and twelve workers instead of three
filling the front yard
all young men
shirtless
and shining black
in the morning sun
muscles rippling

I thought I had died
and gone to man heaven

All day they worked
passing buckets of quickly mixed cement
from ground to roof
swinging them man to man
up the ladder
which served as scaffolding

It took two days
Fascinated
I could not move
The casting of the roof had me spellbound
for two days I forgot
my fight for the environment
I forgot the need for bees
I forgot the feeding of hummingbirds
I forgot the habitat of lizards

On the third day I rose
to an empty yard
no not empty
just manless
and full of concrete

DEPARTURE OF A DAUGHTER

It's early in the morning
and the sky is overcast
I look out to sea
I can see rain in the distance
and the reef is marked
by the white of breaking waves
even the flowers hang their heads
across the gate
and the mango sheds its leaves
I'm not surprised
the sun won't shine
my daughter left this morning
an early bus to Kingston
to catch a flight to Miami
two weeks with auntie and cousin
and then to New York
to meet boyfriend
a summer job in his family restaurant
and then back to Kingston
to write her masters dissertation
she arrives back
one day after I leave for England

I won't see her again
till London in November
I never thought
when I brought her home
a child of five
and rocked her
on this very verandah
that my return
would signal her departure

Back to the land of her birth she says
I use to beg her to sit with me
on the verandah
she preferred the TV room
pasted to the music channel
and her phone
and now she's gone for good

Who's going to tell me
what's at number one in the charts
or which DJ has just burst out on the scene
or how to cut and paste a poem

Yes, the sky is overcast
and it seems fit somehow
it's her turn to travel
as age creeps up on me
I think at her age
I was just the same
I would not have been happy
to just sit on a verandah
but now
the sky
and the changing patterns of the waves
is all the difference I need

AFTER THE WORLD CUP

It's a day of sea breeze
laughing through the mango tree
the world is back to normal
no more hyped-up days
of countries at war on football fields
There is the distant slow pitch
of a cricket commentator's voice
this is summer as we know it
even in the shade
we sweat

My day starts early
with my morning swim
back for breakfast on the verandah
and no one is waiting to see my mother
for that elusive recommendation
for that elusive job
The builders on my sister's house
have taken a week's rest
and I am alone
the crop of mango is over
there are no fruits
falling on the verandah roof
and to the ground
softened by the sudden heavy drop
and ready to wash and eat

The heat is heavy
and the sweat falls to my lap
as I doze and wake
and doze and wake

This is the verandah's quiet day
aroused only by the sea breeze
and traffic
soon the sun will dip
and only an orange glow will fill the sky

On days like these
the world does not enter
the quiet village life
even by TV
It seems a long way from Brazil
which yesterday seemed so close
now everyone has gone back home
to what's left of summer
in the north
and the heat here
closes in

A VISIT FROM SCOTLAND

This rastaman
I do not recognise
but from the confidence of his step
he recognises me

Sista Breeze
yuh come?

Just the Queen I want to see
yuh tink it right, sista
yuh tink it right
for Scotland to ask for freedom?

I am caught somewhere
mid-atlantic
trying to remember where I am coming from
and how to get back home

Who better to ask
than someone who spend so much time in Britain

Yuh really tink it right
for Scotland to ask for freedom?

We did
and look where it land we
squeeze tight by the IMF
and the dolla
not even worth one pence

Scotland should learn from we
independence only sound free
but not actually
what you tink, sista Breeze?

The only freedom is
we don't have to bow to the Queen

I yearn desperately for inspiration
words to quench his desire for an argument

Freedom is for all I say
it's for us to grow with it
but the Scottish people are no fools
they will do what's best for them

He shrugs this off
disappointed by the lack of wisdom in the words

Shaking his head
he strides towards the gate
mumbling as he goes
Scotland, Scotland
Scot free
Not sure, I
not sure

BREAKFAST SURPRISE

My mother surprised me early
with breakfast on the verandah
I am on my second cup of coffee
and she brings
fried dumplings
ackee and saltfish
and fried plantains

There are three of us
around the verandah table
my mother, my stepfather and I
We three live here now
sharing all this space
but the verandah is usually mine
except for the occasional breakfast
my mother chooses to serve here

I am about to put the first bite in my mouth
when my stepfather looks at me deeply
Jean, he says
'if you should die in England
do you want to be buried there,
or shall we bring home your body?'

I choke
the morning sun is shining
its first light on the garden
and my senses are just awakening
to the smell of freshly cooked food
not exactly the question I need to answer
but it seems a serious one
so I try

Bring nothing home I say
cremate
on the spot
and if you want
spread the dust across the sea
I belong to the wind and to the sea
not to worms
or roots of trees

He seems satisfied
and bites into his dumpling

I have to wait
for my appetite to return

BIRTH

I can't remember
which verandah it happened on
but it was a verandah
I remember
I had just returned from school
and the midwife came out of the house
and said
'you have a sister'
so it must have been that first verandah
in the village where I was born
and I was only four
so it must have been

And it was my first sister
four years younger than me
I remember being upset
as I was not allowed into the room
and I wanted to see my mother
but the woman in white
said I had to wait a while

I sat there
swinging my legs over the front steps
wanting to know my sister's name
and to see her face
forgetting I was hungry
no one remembered lunch
and finally
my mother's voice
woke me from my reverie
calling me to come
This is Pam
she said
your new sister
you can't hold her yet

Soon
soon
the room seemed dark
after the verandah
and I asked
could I kiss her
Yes said my mother
but then you have to go
I need some rest
and she needs sleep

Back on that verandah
my father waited too
and it seemed a long way into evening
when they woke
and I remember
there was no light on that verandah
no sea either
in the distance
just a steep hill to the road
but I remember it
well

THE ROCKING CHAIR

It's too late now
for the rocking chair
aunt Vida died
some five years back
at ninety-three
and I hadn't yet
delivered the promised chair
to her special place
on the verandah
she had made herself comfortable
in the wicker basket chair
which became her seat

now no one needs to rock

My mother prefers
a lie down in her room
for a few hours in the afternoon
and I can't write while rocking
I need a steadier seat

When we are young
and fleet of foot
we do not see how quickly
elders pass
when we grow old
and stop to look
we find that suddenly
they're gone

SOUND SYSTEM

There is no need
to play music
on my verandah
being as it is
surrounded on three sides
by bars
who take it in turn
day and night
to play loud enough
for the entire village
or
in lieu of a party
just turn the radio up high

so its sound system
or Irie FM
and there's bound to be something
pleasing to everyone
except perhaps
the Christian
whose numbers my mother makes up

So she does not come
to the verandah very much
and I am left
to make heads or tails of it
while she shuts her door
and turns on the TV
or reads the Bible loudly
inspired by
God
and the gospel channel

TWEET TWEET

There's a blackbird
in my mango tree
and I think of Marley
and singing songs of freedom

I have followed birds
from hills
to home
and back
wondering where was Zion

but now I am content
on this verandah

the blackbirds come to my mango tree
and sing

home is always
where it's meant to be

I am sure
that's what blackbirds sing

HEAT

It's six a.m.
and it's the first cup of coffee
on the verandah
the street sweepers are out
and the traffic is building slowly
already the sky takes on
its first blushes of colour
from the sun
like a woman takes on her make-up
in the morning
the sea is quiet
no wind
no breaking waves
and suddenly I realise
what is missing
the voices
there are no children's voices
waking up the day
it's July
and school is out
the children sleep late
and their buses are not running

What comes quickly now in the morning
is the heat
summer is at its height
even now
yesterday's heat seems to linger
not cleared by the cool of night
and early morning sweat
comes with the coffee
there is only one solution
to strip to shorts
and dive into the sea

It is warm
even in the morning sea
but for an hour or two
it makes the day possible
hopefully the wind will pick up
sea breezes will rise with the day
and back on the verandah
wearing some cool cotton
the rain clouds may come early

By lunch time
if we're lucky
the thunder of the early afternoon
will break the sky
and the rain smell of the earth
will cool us humans down
and maybe
just maybe
night will not come
with the anger
of heated arguments

NEW MEN

Things aren't what they used to be
years ago
when I was young
sitting on this same verandah
only women
walked with children
babies, toddlers, or early teens
young men walked together
in groups
wearing football boots
or carrying spear guns to go fishing

but now
young men carry babies
precious dear things
trembling on their chests
or holding them comfortably
above the shoulders
alongside the bag with the necessaries
or holding hands
with those who could walk
stopping to pick them flowers
growing over the wall
from our front garden
no
things aren't what they used to be
young men have become new men
no longer do they feel
these duties are for women

in fact
the rasta man
across the road
does all of this
and even dyes his hair

LOCKING THE DOOR

It's two a.m.
and there's a cat
sat
on the hot tin roof
next door
the distant sultry sound of reggae
dubs the night
and the music is broken
by screams

three young men
run pass the gate
hurling stones
at the one who dodges in the bush

I think it is a bar fight
but then the young girl runs across the road
into the yard
and faces me
on the verandah
her head bleeds

the young men disappear
and the one that they are stoning
follows her to my gate
then stops

'Whore', he shouts
'whore'

and I recognise him
as the madman
who prowls the street at day

I pull her inside
and say
let's call the police
but she runs out the door
shouting no
they'll send me home
I am a gogo dancer
and I am under age

she runs to the back of the house
and into the bush beyond
the madman follows her
I call the police anyway

It is nearly an hour
before they show up
an hour of me watching
and the madman coming again to the gate
the sound of the police car moves him
I wait awhile
and walk to the car
parked across the road
I tell them all that happened
and point to the bushes
where both have now disappeared
they get back into the car
and drive away
the bush is not safe at night they say
could step into a crab hole
and break a leg

Now there's no one on the street
the dub continues its distant beat
but
the verandah feels unsafe
I retreat to my bed
making sure
to lock the door

For forty years
we've lived in this house
without a secure lock

young men are going mad they say
young men are going mad
they say it's no more ganja
young men have turned to crack

DOROTHY

When it's time to clean the kitchen
my mother and I change places
she cooks
I clean
she calls from the verandah
Jean!
I hear my name shouted through the door
my children and friends call me Binta
but my mother calls me Jean

You have a visitor she says

I wash my hands
and make my way
from the dark of the kitchen
to the sunlit verandah

My god! Dorothy, I don't believe it!
my mother says
I forgot to tell you yesterday she called

Dorothy!
my two lives are met on the verandah

Dorothy my friend
who invited me to try Leicester
when I was looking for a place to live in England
ten years I spent there
just across the park from her
and here she is
on my front verandah
this calls for the best
of my mother's june plum juice
and many glasses filled with ice
to combat the heat

Dorothy has brought
her Jamaican family with her

How long will you stay

Just today

Not possible I say
at least overnight

We made no plans

No plans are necessary my mother says
the rooms are ready
you are welcome

And then begins the long talk into night
catching up on both sides of the Atlantic
my mother replaces me in the kitchen
and we can smell the spices
of home-cooked Jamaican specialties

but friends are like that
they turn up from the other side of the world
and nothing has changed
except
we are both a little fatter
and if my mother has anything to do with it
our waistlines will continue to spread.

RAINBOW MORNING

There is a rainbow in the sky today
colours across the sea
with last night's rain left over
in the darkened skies
to the west
and the morning sun now rising
over the mountains
in the east
the sky now tells the story
of December's windy weather
and the coming cool of January
like the best of an English summer

There is a rainbow in the sky today
a reason to wake with the sun
all day long
will be bright and then shady
till the evening story is done
and the night
kisses us with stardom

NO GHOST

I dreamt last night
that I was sitting
with my father
on the verandah
drinking rum
it was a strange dream
as I was in school uniform
and way too young
to be imbibing rum

he certainly would not have let me
yet, when I was 13, he opened the door wider
and called me from the kitchen
to bring his bottle
and his choice of drinking cup,
aluminium, he chose
he could let it drop
and it would not break
only dent
and it was not glass
so no one could see
how much he poured himself

That afternoon came back
my first taste of rum
mingled with the dream
at 3 in the morning
when I woke
sweating
I could smell rum
so I opened the door
to the verandah
and stepped out
sure I would meet my father
but not afraid of his ghost

He was not a happy man
in his rum
yet all he asked of me
was to be quick
bringing his ice and water
and that I poured
just the right amount
so the mix
was perfect to his tongue

But that night
there was no ghost of my father
on the verandah
only the barking
of the neighbour's dog
as I disturbed the night

And one lone drunk
hobbling along
the last man from the rum bar up the road
walking in the direction
of the cemetery

TSUNAMI

The verandah of the bar across the road
is within shouting distance

the bar itself sits almost in the sea

I watch waves break
on the reef beyond
and call out loud
good morning to the King
and my voice is so strong
in conversation
across the road
despite the years of smoke
so strong
that I think
if there is ever a tsunami
I will shout

BACK OFF

and we shall be saved
we will watch the wave
turn
and return
to ocean
from whence it came

RUM

I poured a rum
on the verandah
this afternoon
in honour of my father
forgetting the advice of my doctors
to avoid strong alcohol

I am sure
they would have given my father
the same advice
if he had thought to visit them
he went to the doctors once
the week before he died

My mother has thrown out
his aluminium cups
so I am drinking from a glass
and I am drinking it with water
as he advised
never poison your rum
by adding more sugar to cane

As I drink the rum
I know it is probably my last
I could feel the swelling of my head
it does not sit well
with my medication
Ay! It is a sad day
when you find yourself retired
in rum country
and not able to swallow
the spirit of the land

VISITATION

Dawta, he shouts from the road
Can come?

His eyes circle the garden
the mango tree
my mother's home

In a few strides
he is at the verandah
Ah so mi like see rasta live
yuh know!
In a nice house
set back from di road
wid a pretty flowers garden

No half way inna street
no zinc sheet tenement
nor no hut in the deepest bush

So mi like see rasta house
nicely painted
and the verandah wide
a comfortable seat up
fi de empress

But Queen I
you look lonely
siddung by yuhself

So what?
I king man free yuh know
I king man free to move in
today

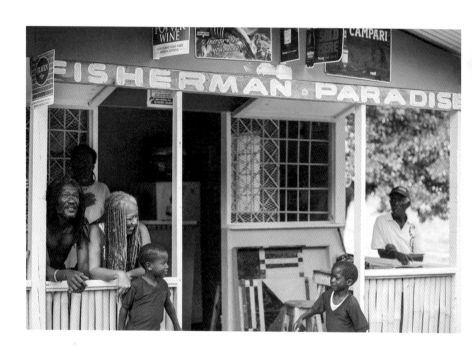

RED, GOLD AND GREEN

It is two days to Christmas
and the rastaman is painting

The red is to the ground
up a bit to gold
and the green flies high

He says
is because he runs a place of love
if he flies the red on top
he would mean war
but that is not his intention

This year,
he could not find the same colour gold
so it is milder yellow in the centre
but then he says
the dollar's weak
is not a golden Christmas
but the love is strong
Queen I
the love is strong

There is no war in the house
the children are fed
and the brethren gather in reasoning
the drought has ended
and the rains have come again
and now the sun is back
just for Christmas

We will catch fish on Christmas Eve
and they will grace our feast
in fisherman's paradise
on Jah's special day

PIERCINGS

I sit here
looking out
as the car
with my daughters
arrives from the beach
They step out
belly buttons and bikinis
shimmering in the sun

When I was nine
the senator's daughter
arrived back from England
with the magic spray
that deadens flesh
and she pierced my ears

How I begged my daughters
not to pierce their belly buttons
the same way my mother begged me
not to pierce my ears

It's a long passage of years
from the ear
to the belly button

CHRISTMAS EVE

My sister's house
no longer houses her
It is a shop
no, a boutique
She has come from America
and stocked it
with clothes and shoes
She is sorry now
she bought so much for women
it is the young men who swarm the shop
buying their floral tracksuit bottomed pants
and designer shirts
They are spending money
the lady in the shop says

Dese days, pum pum don't wort a ting
young bwoy ah carry di swing
dem a scam an do dem ting
Christmas Eve dem goh pan a fling

My sista says
she made more than one year's rent
in a single night

CHRISMUS

Bwoy,
this wasn't no cold outside
wrap up warm
eat no turkey
Chrismus

Wasn't no
late night shopping
whole heap a light pon tree
spen two hours
wid mom and dad
Chrismus

Dis was
di whole family
and fi dem family
come een week before
empty the food store
cook and eat
cook and eat
and save di bes
fi di chrismus day treat
kind a chrismus

Dis was a sleep fi two day after
den end up pon di beach
wid some roast fish
Chrismus

Dis was a pack up pan di verandah
late in the evening
and tell story to the pickney dem
and listen to the elders
talk bout
Chrismus

Dis was a everybody lef
one week later
house empty
me one pon di verandah again
remembering
anadda Chrismus

PRESENTS

We opened our presents
on the verandah
having just arrived back
from Christmas morning carol service
and set the breadfruits to roast
for breakfast

My daughter hands me a package
which is obviously a bottle
and I am full of depression
no, not a bottle of rum
or some other spirit
Didn't I tell them what the doctor said?
but I must look cheerful
so, I smiled and opened it
It is ginger wine
well at least it is weak enough
to finish in one day

As I say a big thank you
she slides a box across the table
and says
Mum, open that for me
I do as she asks
no longer interested in presents

It is a phone

Switch it on, she says
Her husband smiles beside her
and in that one touch
they have moved me into the 21st century

I
the technophobe
no computer
no internet
no Facebook page
one little cheap plastic phone
just learnt to send a text

Yes, I switched it on
on the screen
is a picture of my three children
Just touch it once
she says
I do
and opened up a world
of internet
and Skype
and whatsapp

I opened up a world
across the world
of continuous conversations
conducted from my verandah
across the Atlantic
the Pacific
I watch my grandchildren play
half way across the world
at a touch of the screen
My daughter has set up everything I need
at a touch
I never knew it could be so easy

It is a smartphone, Mum
she says
Just touch
don't be afraid to touch

NEW YEAR'S EVE

Seven o'clock New Year's Eve
It is twelve midnight in London
I must dial quickly
and keep my calls short
so many family and friends
that side of the water

Tonight
I don't want messaging
I want the warmth of voices
the joy of speech
the feel of New Year's greetings

Now after all that
I have to dress
wait for my lift
to be early
on my friend's verandah
overlooking Montego Bay

I pack a bag
of excess drink
give myself a choice
to lead me up to midnight

Nothing sits well on my stomach this evening
oh, how I miss my rum

A new drink, I think
for the New Year
so I settle for glasses
of vodka and ting
the tangy grapefruit soda
they glide down easily
hour after hour, packed with ice

My friend Dona's sister,
who is a Joy,
plays the old hits
that go with New Year's Eve
it's an evening of sing a long
and at midnight
we watched the fireworks explode
round the city below
and the hotels in the distance

How I start my New Year matters
this is my third year
with Philip
and still no copulation
he says it will be his last
if I don't submit

For me
it is the welcome
of another year of celibacy
still the old hits play

'searching so long, just for you'

And I wish I could save him
with a dance
hold him close under the moonlight
on the lawn
but how to do that
without promising
what I won't deliver
I keep my distance
we sing along till morning

Old hits
taking me all the way home
for a New Year
still at ease
on my verandah

Jean 'Binta' Breeze is a poet, actress, dancer, choreographer, film writer and theatre director. She has released seven poetry books, *Riddym Ravings* (Race Today, 1988), *Spring Cleaning* (Virago, 1992), and *On the Edge of an Island* (1997), *The Arrival of Brighteye* (2000), *The Fifth Figure* (2006), *Third World Girl: Selected Poems* (2011, with DVD) and *The Verandah Poems* (2016) with Bloodaxe, as well as several records and CDs, including *Tracks* and *Eena Me Corner* with the Dennis Bovell Dub Band and *Riding On De Riddym: selected spoken works* (57 Productions). She has performed her work throughout the world, including tours of the Caribbean, Britain, North America, Europe, South East Asia and Africa, and now divides her time between Jamaica and England. She received a NESTA Award in 2003.